SIMPLY THE BEST
STEAMER RECIPES

MARIAN GETZ

INTRODUCTION BY WOLFGANG PUCK

AS I LEARNED LONG AGO, ALONGSIDE MY MOTHER AND GRANDMOTHER, YOU SHOULD ALWAYS PUT LOTS OF LOVE INTO EVERYTHING YOU COOK. THIS IS CERTAINLY EVIDENT IN THIS COOKBOOK.

Wolfgang Puck

Most of us think of steaming food as a practice mostly used for preparing Asian dishes such as rice, pot stickers, vegetables and fish. Many of my restaurants use steamers for their versatility and simplicity. I created a steamer for the home cook to use and enjoy on an everyday basis and I have urged Marian to share her favorite recipes with as many people as possible through this cookbook.

Marian was thrilled to write a cookbook to accompany the steamer. She instantly thought of dozens of recipes to include in this cookbook. Steaming can be universal throughout all cooking cultures and she used her knowledge to create recipes for any occasion.

When I asked Marian to write the cookbook for the steamer, I knew she would rise to the occasion. Her experience as a pastry chef, wife, mother, and grandmother allowed Marian to put together a cookbook with a wide variety of recipes that I'm sure you will use for years to come.

A student of cooking is probably one of the best ways to describe Marian. She is always looking for something new, something fresh, something local, something seasonal. Her culinary knowledge combined with her passion for cooking is second to none. The recipes that Marian has written for this cookbook will motivate you to be more creative in the kitchen.

TABLE OF CONTENTS

TABLE OF CONTENTS

STEAMER TIPS

Steamer Baskets

The number of steamer baskets to use for a given recipe depends on the size of the food and how it is cut. For this reason, most recipes will state to place the food into a steamer basket, with the instruction to use additional steamer baskets if needed. So depending on your situation, use as many as needed to fit all your food. Some of the recipes state specifically how many steamer baskets to use, just follow the instructions for best results.

Water Reservoir

Before using the steamer, fill the Water Reservoir to the MAX line as indicated on the Water Level Window using cold water. Do not overfill the Water Reservoir above the MAX line and never allow the water level to fall below the MIN line to prevent damage to your steamer. Water can be added during the steaming process via the Drip Tray Water Spout.

Hot Steam

Please use caution when removing the covers from the steamer baskets. Use thick oven mitts to protect your hands and forearms. Steam burns happen fast and are very painful.

Kitchen Towels

After steaming is complete, there will be considerable moisture left which might damage your kitchen counter. To protect against this, have ready a kitchen towel or paper towels for placing the steamer baskets when removing them after steaming is complete.

Additional Steaming Time

Food size, density and temperature can differ so steaming times may vary from the suggested steaming time in the recipes. If the food you are steaming is not done at the suggested steaming time, add a few more minutes to the timer. Depending on the length of time you have already been steaming, you may have to add more water to the steamer as well.

Rice Bowl

The rice bowl refers to the bowl-like container that comes with your steamer and is placed inside the steamer basket. It is very good for steaming juicy items or very small items that would otherwise fall through the grates of the steamer such as rice.

Placing and Removing Items from Steamer Baskets

When placing foods into the steamer baskets, make sure not to cover all of the steam holes in the bottom as this might affect steaming performance and steaming time. Don't pack foods into steamer baskets too densely to allow the steam to freely flow around the food to ensure even steaming. When placing ramekins into the steamer baskets, space them out evenly without stacking. The best way to remove ramekins from the steamer baskets is to use a thin pancake turner to get under the ramekins while keeping your hands away from the hot steam.

Testing for Doneness

One of the most frequently asked questions I am asked is: "is it done?" Almost all of cooking is a judgement call but there are many clues that will help you know when something is just right and fully cooked.

Fish and shellfish will lose translucency as they are cooked and are done when white and slightly firm to the touch.

To check baked goods for doneness, they should be firm to the touch. Alternatively, you can test for doneness by inserting a wooden pick off-center, it should generally come out with just a few moist crumbs clinging to it. You can also use a thermometer which should register approximately 200°F when done.

For custards, they will "wobble" when tapped on the side of the ramekin or whichever vessel they were steamed in. You can also insert a knife off-center and it should come out clean.

Potatoes or sweet potatoes are done once soft when squeezed.

For raw proteins such as beef, poultry or pork, we've mostly been taught by our parents and grandparents to check for doneness by cutting into it to check for a non-pink color as well as clear juices without any traces of pink or red. While this method still works, a meat thermometer is a more accurate way to check for doneness and for preventing over or under cooking which can ruin expensive meats.

A good meat thermometer registers the temperature quickly and has a "cheat sheet" on the back for quick reference. I recommend using an instant-read thermometer (see source page on page 109).

Brining Meats

There are recipes in this book that use a brine before steaming. Brining completely flavors the meat throughout and pulls in moisture. While this is an added step, it can be left unattended and is well worth it for the benefit of flavor and juiciness. This step can be skipped if you are pressed for time. It is especially helpful to brine meats if you have a spouse or family member that is not too excited about any new, healthy recipes you might be preparing for them from your steamer. The pork chop recipes in this book won my husband over. He was not particularly excited to eat a steamed meal until he tasted how flavorful brined meats from the steamer can be.

Color of Steamed Foods

Vegetables become stunningly beautiful when steamed unlike meats and baked goods. For meats, one of the best ways to improve the color is by adding a rub or using spices. Unlike cooking in a hot pan on the stove, adding oils does not enhance browning while steaming. Any added oils will run off the meat and end up in the drip tray of the steamer. Breads or other baked goods will be naturally pale in color compared to being baked in the oven. The pale color is not an indication that the baked goods are undercooked, it is just a result of cooking using steam.

Raw Protein

When cooking raw protein such as beef, poultry, fish, shellfish and pork, be mindful of what you do with your tongs. If you use the same pair of tongs to place raw protein into the steamer baskets then later use them to transfer the cooked protein to a platter, there is a chance that those tongs may still have live bacteria on them. Either wash them before removing cooked food or use a second pair.

Seasoning Your Food

When cooking savory foods, it is important to season it first. It can be as simple as salt alone or an elaborate array of spices and herbs. Season EVERY BITE of the food by sprinkling the seasonings evenly over the surface of the food. For me, salt and pepper do not always go together. Salt is by far the most important seasoning followed by something tart such as citrus, vinegar, wine, BBQ sauce or mustard that has a tartness to it. It's all about the right balance.

Prep Once - Use Twice

Think about any meals you may want to cook during the upcoming week and prep for more than you need today. For example, if you're chopping vegetables for today's meal, can you use them later in the week? If so, prep extra today and save time tomorrow.

Salt

The salt used in this book is Diamond Crystal Kosher Salt. It is half as salty as most other brands. This is because the grains are very fluffy and therefore not as many fit into a measuring spoon. This brand also lists only "salt" as the ingredient which is great. Most other brand have ingredients that are not natural and ruin the taste. If you are using salt other than Diamond Crystal Kosher Salt, simply use approximately half the amount specified in the recipe. Smoked salts, available in many grocery stores and online, are a great way to add flavor to steamed foods as well. Try the steamed edamame with smoked salt recipe on page 98.

Butter

If a recipe calls for butter, I always use the unsalted kind. Salted butter has a longer shelf life as the salt acts as a preservative but it comes at the expense of a taste that is stale compared to that of unsalted butter. Softened butter means butter that has been left at room temperature for several hours. It should be soft enough to offer no resistance whatsoever when sliced using a knife. While there is no perfect substitute for the pure flavor of butter, you can use a substitute such as vegan butter, coconut oil or margarine and most of the recipes will turn out fairly well.

Vanilla

I adore vanilla and order both my vanilla extract and vanilla beans from a supplier directly from the island of Tahiti. I use both of these in recipes where the vanilla flavor takes center stage. In recipes where vanilla is not the star flavor, I use imitation vanilla because it is less expensive and adds the right amount of taste and aroma without overpowering the other flavors.

Sugar Substitute

While substitutes do not bake as perfectly as regular sugar, they are ok to use if you prefer them.

Chocolate

Buy good quality chocolate and cocoa whenever possible. It is easy to find excellent chocolate at most grocery stores but it is almost impossible to find good quality cocoa powder. Please see the source page 109 for places online to buy good quality cocoa powder.

PANTRY TIPS

Being prepared to cook or bake the recipes in this book, or any recipe for that matter, is one of the keys to success in the kitchen. Your pantry must be stocked with the basics. We all know how frustrating it can be when you go to the cupboard and what you need is not there. This list includes some of the ingredients you will find in this book and some that I feel are important to always have on hand.

PERISHABLES	SPICES	DRY GOODS	FREEZER
Dark Leafy Greens	Kosher Salt	Flours	Frozen Fruits
Zucchini	Fresh Peppercorn	Sugar	Frozen Vegetables
Carrots	Bay Leaves	Sugar Substitutes	Bao Buns
Yellow Squash	Sage	Rice	Rhubarb
Onions	Oregano	Pasta	Edamame
Butternut Squash	Thyme	Quinoa	Shrimp
Apples	Chili Flakes	Sriracha	Fish
Pears	Cumin Seeds	Chocolate	Kale
White Potatoes	Curry Powder	Honey	Spinach
Sweet Potatoes	Onion Powder	Oils	Broccoli
Green Onions	Garlic Powder	Pickles	Cauliflower
Garlic	Dry Mustard	Bouillon Bases	
Ginger	Ground Cinnamon	Canned Tomatoes	
Herbs	Nutmeg	Extracts/Flavorings	
Tomatoes	Cloves	Vinegars	
Greens	Chili Powder		
Milk/Nut Milks			
Cheese/Vegan Cheese			
Yogurt/Non-Dairy Yogurt			
Eggs			

It is not necessary to have all the items listed at all times. However, if you are feeling creative, adventurous or just following a recipe, it's great to have a good selection in the kitchen.

BBQ CHICKEN
DINNER

Makes 2 servings

Ingredients:

2 boneless, skinless chicken breasts, raw

Kosher salt and fresh pepper to taste

6 petite red bliss potatoes, quartered

1 cob yellow corn, halved

2 handfuls green beans

1 tablespoon unsalted butter, melted

1/3 cup bottled BBQ sauce

Method:

1. *Fill the water reservoir with cold water up to the MAX line, fit with drip tray then add steamer basket.*
2. *Season chicken and all vegetables with salt and pepper.*
3. *Place all ingredients, except butter and BBQ sauce, into steamer basket and cover (use additional steamer baskets if needed).*
4. *Set timer knob to 12 minutes.*
5. *Steam for 12 minutes or until chicken and potatoes are just cooked through.*
6. *When steaming is complete, transfer to a serving plate.*
7. *Drizzle butter over the vegetables then season with additional salt and pepper if desired.*
8. *Spoon BBQ sauce over chicken and serve.*

Simple Steamed Potatoes
(See page 47)

PESTO STEAMED SALMON

Makes 2 servings

Ingredients:

1 medium yellow onion, sliced into rings

2 salmon fillets

Kosher salt and fresh pepper to taste

2 tablespoons store-bought pesto + more for serving

1 lemon, sliced into wheels

4 cups fresh baby spinach (optional)

Method:

1. *Fill the water reservoir with cold water up to the MAX line, fit with drip tray then add steamer basket.*
2. *Place onions into steamer basket.*
3. *Season salmon with salt and pepper on all sides then place on top of onions into the steamer basket.*
4. *Spread a tablespoon of pesto over each salmon fillet.*
5. *Place a lemon wheel on top of each fillet then cover.*
6. *Set timer knob to 6 minutes.*
7. *Steam for 6 minutes or until just cooked through.*
8. *If desired, add spinach to the steamer basket during the last 2 minutes of steaming.*
9. *When steaming is complete, remove, garnish as desired and serve.*

EASY
EGG CUPS

Makes 3 servings

Ingredients:

1 cup baby spinach

1/4 bell pepper, chopped

2 tablespoons ricotta cheese

2 large eggs

1 green onion, chopped

1/4 cup Cheddar cheese, shredded

Kosher salt and fresh pepper to taste

Method:

1. *Fill the water reservoir with cold water up to the MAX line, fit with drip tray then add steamer basket.*
2. *In a mixing bowl, whisk together all ingredients then divide between 3 small ramekins.*
3. *Place ramekins into steamer basket and cover.*
4. *Set timer knob to 12 minutes.*
5. *Steam for 12 minutes or until eggs are just set or desired doneness is achieved.*
6. *When steaming is complete, remove, garnish as desired and serve.*

CHOCOLATE MUG CAKE
FOR ONE

Makes 1 mug cake

Ingredients:

3 tablespoons whole milk

1 large egg

3 tablespoons vegetable oil

1/4 teaspoon vanilla extract

3 tablespoons all purpose flour

4 tablespoons granulated sugar

2 tablespoons cocoa powder

A pinch of kosher salt

3 tablespoons chocolate chips

Method:

1. Place all ingredients into a mug then stir using a fork until blended.
2. Fill the water reservoir with cold water up to the MAX line, fit with drip tray then add steamer basket.
3. Place mug into steamer basket and cover.
4. Set timer knob to 12 minutes.
5. Steam for 12 minutes or until wobbly at the center.
6. When steaming is complete, remove, garnish as desired and serve.

PORK CHOPS WITH APPLE BUTTER

Makes 2 servings

Ingredients:

4 cups cold water

3 tablespoons kosher salt (or 1 1/2 tablespoons other salt)

1 tablespoon fresh pepper

2 pork chops, 1-inch thick

2 tart apples, cut into wedges

1/2 cup jarred apple butter

1 tablespoon balsamic vinegar

Method:

1. *In a mixing bowl, combine the water, salt and pepper; whisk until dissolved.*
2. *Place pork chops into the brine then cover with plastic wrap.*
3. *Place bowl in the refrigerator for 1 hour.*
4. *Fill the water reservoir with cold water up to the MAX line, fit with drip tray then add 2 steamer baskets.*
5. *Place pork chops into one steamer basket and cover.*
6. *Set timer knob to 12 minutes.*
7. *Steam for 12 minutes or until pork is just cooked through.*
8. *While pork chops are steaming, place apples into second steamer basket and cover.*
9. *Set timer knob to 8 minutes.*
10. *When steaming is complete, transfer all to serving plates.*
11. *Stir together the apple butter and balsamic vinegar then brush on both sides of each pork chop.*
12. *Drizzle any remaining apple butter mixture over apples before serving.*

TIP
You can skip the brining step
if you don't have time.

CURRY CHICKEN BREASTS

Makes 2 servings

Ingredients:

Kosher salt to taste

1 tablespoon curry powder

1 teaspoon ground turmeric

2 boneless, skinless chicken breasts, raw

2 cups green beans (optional)

Method:

1. *On a plate, combine the salt, curry and turmeric.*
2. *Dip both sides of chicken breasts in curry mixture using a fork.*
3. *Fill the water reservoir with cold water up to the MAX line, fit with drip tray then add steamer basket.*
4. *Place chicken into steamer basket and cover.*
5. *Set timer knob to 12 minutes.*
6. *Steam for 12 minutes or until cooked through.*
7. *If desired, add green beans during last 5 minutes of steaming.*
8. *When steaming is complete, remove, garnish as desired and serve.*

STEAMED HOT DOGS &
SAUERKRAUT

Makes 4 servings

Ingredients:

4 jumbo hot dogs

2 cups sauerkraut

4 hot dog buns

Condiments of your choice, for serving

Method:

1. *Fill the water reservoir with cold water up to the MAX line, fit with drip tray then add 3 steamer baskets.*
2. *Place hot dogs into one steamer basket.*
3. *Place sauerkraut into rice bowl then place into second steamer basket.*
4. *Cover both then set each timer knob to 8 minutes.*
5. *Steam hot dogs and sauerkraut for 8 minutes or until heated through.*
6. *Place hot dog buns into third steamer basket, cover and briefly steam for 20 seconds right before serving.*
7. *When steaming is complete, carefully remove buns, sauerkraut and hot dogs.*
8. *Assemble hot dogs with desired condiments and serve.*

SKINNY STEAMED GREENS

Makes 2 servings

Ingredients:

1 bunch fresh kale, turnip greens or collard greens, washed and torn

1 cup vegetable stock, heated

1 teaspoon liquid smoke (optional)

1/2 teaspoon chili flakes or hot sauce

1 teaspoon apple cider vinegar

Kosher salt and fresh pepper to taste

Method:

1. *Fill the water reservoir with cold water up to the MAX line, fit with drip tray then add 3 steamer baskets.*
2. *Divide greens between all 3 steamer baskets and cover.*
3. *Set timer knobs to 6 minutes.*
4. *Steam for 6 minutes or until crisp tender.*
5. *When steaming is complete, transfer to a serving bowl.*
6. *Add remaining ingredients to the bowl and stir.*
7. *Garnish as desired and serve.*

TIP

It is best to use all three steamer baskets for these greens to achieve even steaming as they drastically reduce in size during steaming.

STEAM BAKED APPLES

Makes 2 servings

Ingredients:

2 Granny Smith apples

1 tablespoon dark raisins

2 tablespoons brown sugar or other sweetener

1 teaspoon ground cinnamon

A small pinch of kosher salt

1/2 teaspoon vanilla extract

Method:

1. *Using a melon baller, carefully remove stem and seeds from each apple without piercing the bottom of each apple.*
2. *In a small bowl, stir together remaining ingredients.*
3. *Fill each apple cavity with raisin mixture.*
4. *Fill the water reservoir with cold water up to the MAX line, fit with drip tray then add steamer basket.*
5. *Place apples into steamer basket and cover.*
6. *Set timer knob to 20 minutes.*
7. *Steam for 20 minutes or until apples are soft when squeezed with a towel.*
8. *When steaming is complete, remove carefully as the center will be hot and liquid.*
9. *Garnish as desired and serve hot or warm.*

CRÈME BRÛLÉE

Makes 2 servings

Ingredients:

1 cup heavy cream

2 tablespoons granulated sugar

1 teaspoon vanilla extract

3 large egg yolks

A pinch of kosher salt

Additional granulated sugar, for burning tops

Method:

1. *In a bowl, whisk together all ingredients, except additional sugar, until thoroughly combined.*
2. *Evenly divide mixture between 2 ramekins.*
3. *Fill the water reservoir with cold water up to the MAX line, fit with drip tray then add steamer basket.*
4. *Place ramekins into steamer basket and cover.*
5. *Set timer knob to 14 minutes.*
6. *Steam for 14 minutes or until wobbly and just set when tapped.*
7. *When steaming is complete, transfer ramekins to a cookie sheet.*
8. *Sprinkle each top with a thin, even layer of sugar.*
9. *Use a blow torch (see source page 109) to caramelize the sugar.*
10. *Sprinkle with a second even layer of sugar.*
11. *Use the blow torch to caramelize the second layer of sugar.*
12. *Let sugar cool for 5 minutes before serving.*

HARD BOILED
EGGS

Makes 6 eggs

Ingredients:

6 large eggs

Method:

1. *Fill the water reservoir with cold water up to the MAX line, fit with drip tray then add steamer basket.*
2. *Place eggs into steamer basket and cover.*
3. *Set timer knob to 12 minutes.*
4. *When steaming is complete, remove eggs then crack shells all over.*
5. *Peel eggs under a hard stream of cold water from the faucet.*
6. *Use as desired.*

TIP

Steam eggs for about 7 minutes if
you prefer soft boiled eggs.

BBQ SALMON DINNER

Makes 2 servings

Ingredients:

2 salmon fillets

1 Russet potato, thinly sliced

1/2 head broccoli, cut into florets

1 cup grape tomatoes

Kosher salt and fresh pepper to taste

1/3 cup bottled BBQ sauce

Method:

1. *Fill the water reservoir with cold water up to the MAX line, fit with drip tray then add steamer basket.*
2. *Season salmon and all vegetables with salt and pepper.*
3. *Place all ingredients, except BBQ sauce, into steamer basket and cover (use additional steamer baskets if needed).*
4. *Set timer knob to 6 minutes.*
5. *Steam for 6 minutes or until salmon is just cooked through and potatoes are tender.*
6. *When steaming is complete, transfer to a serving platter.*
7. *Season vegetables with additional salt and pepper if desired.*
8. *Spoon BBQ sauce over salmon before serving.*

APPLE BABY FOOD

Makes 2-4 servings

Ingredients:

1 apple, quartered and seeded

Method:

1. *Fill the water reservoir with cold water up to the MAX line, fit with drip tray then add steamer basket.*
2. *Place apple wedges into steamer basket and cover.*
3. *Set timer knob to 20 minutes.*
4. *Steam for 20 minutes or until very soft to the touch.*
5. *When steaming is complete, transfer to a blender or food processor.*
6. *Blend until smooth, let cool and serve.*

TIP

If you don't have a blender or food processor, you can use an inexpensive manual baby food grinder (see source page 109).

Organic Apple
Baby Food
2/10

Apple
2/10

Apple 2/10

BEST STEAMED
SHRIMP

Makes 2 servings

Ingredients:

For the Shrimp:

1 pound large shrimp, thawed, peeled and deveined

4 cups cold water

1 cup ice cubes

3 tablespoons kosher salt (or 1 1/2 tablespoons other salt)

For the Mustard Sauce:

2 tablespoons spicy brown mustard

2 tablespoons sour cream or yogurt

2 tablespoons apple cider vinegar

Kosher salt and fresh pepper to taste

1 small garlic clove, minced

2 tablespoons fresh parsley, chopped

Method:

1. *Combine all shrimp ingredients in a large bowl.*
2. *Stir to dissolve the salt and let rest for 45 minutes.*
3. *Fill the water reservoir with cold water up to the MAX line, fit with drip tray then add steamer basket.*
4. *Place shrimp into steamer basket and cover.*
5. *Set timer knob to 4 minutes.*
6. *Steam for 4 minutes or until pink and just cooked through.*
7. *While steaming, stir together all sauce ingredients in a small bowl; set aside.*
8. *When steaming is complete, transfer shrimp to a serving platter.*
9. *Serve shrimp with mustard sauce.*

CHICKEN LETTUCE WRAPS

Makes 2 servings

Ingredients:

For the Lettuce Wraps:

8 ounces ground chicken

Kosher salt and fresh pepper to taste

2 green onions, chopped

1 can (7 ounces) diced water chestnuts, drained

4 white mushrooms, diced

1 carrot, diced

For the Sauce:

1 teaspoon dark sesame oil

1 garlic clove, minced

2 teaspoons rice wine vinegar

4 tablespoons hoisin sauce

For Serving:

Iceberg lettuce cups

Method:

1. *Fill the water reservoir with cold water up to the MAX line, fit with drip tray then add steamer basket.*
2. *Place all lettuce wrap ingredients into the rice bowl and stir.*
3. *Place rice bowl into steamer basket and cover.*
4. *Set timer knob to 10 minutes.*
5. *Steam for 10 minutes or until chicken is cooked through.*
6. *When steaming is complete, transfer to a serving bowl.*
7. *Combine all sauce ingredients in a small microwave-safe bowl then heat in microwave for 1 minute.*
8. *Stir sauce into chicken mixture.*
9. *Garnish as desired then serve in lettuce cups.*

TIP

Lettuce wraps are a great way to use up any leftover vegetables you might have on hand. To make it a more filling meal, you can also add some of the steamed rice from page 80.

EASY
BBQ RIBS

Makes 2 servings

Ingredients:

1 slab baby back ribs, sliced into individual ribs

Dry store-bought BBQ rub, enough to coat ribs

Bottled BBQ sauce, for serving

Method:

1. *Place ribs into a large plastic zipper top bag then add the dry rub.*
2. *Shake to evenly coat ribs.*
3. *Fill the water reservoir with cold water up to the MAX line, fit with drip tray then add steamer basket.*
4. *Place ribs approximately 1/2-inch apart into steamer basket without stacking and cover (use additional steamer baskets if needed).*
5. *Set timer knob to 30 minutes.*
6. *Steam for 30 minutes or until ribs are tender.*
7. *When steaming is complete, transfer to a serving platter.*
8. *Brush BBQ sauce over ribs before serving.*

TIP

For a more caramelized rib, broil in the oven for 2-3 minutes after brushing with BBQ sauce.

EASY
QUINOA

Makes 2 servings

Ingredients:

1/2 cup quinoa of your choice

1 cup vegetable stock, boiling

Kosher salt to taste (optional)

Method:

1. *Fill the water reservoir with cold water up to the MAX line, fit with drip tray then add steamer basket.*
2. *Place all ingredients into the rice bowl and stir.*
3. *Place rice bowl into steamer basket and cover.*
4. *Set timer knob to 30 minutes.*
5. *Steam for 30 minutes or until tender.*
6. *When steaming is complete, remove, garnish as desired and serve.*

TIP

The quinoa in the photo is tri-color quinoa but you can use any kind of quinoa you desire.

MEXICAN-STYLE
CORN ON THE COB

Makes 2 servings

Ingredients:

2 ears of corn

2 tablespoons mayonnaise

2 tablespoons Cotija or Parmesan cheese, grated

2 teaspoons ground red chile pepper

Kosher salt to taste

Lime wedges, for serving

Method:

1. *Fill the water reservoir with cold water up to the MAX line, fit with drip tray then add steamer basket.*
2. *Place corn into steamer basket and cover.*
3. *Set timer knob to 5 minutes.*
4. *Steam for 5 minutes or until kernels are tender.*
5. *When steaming is complete, transfer to serving plates.*
6. *Brush each cob with mayonnaise then sprinkle evenly with cheese, chile and salt.*
7. *Squeeze lime over cobs before serving.*

SPICY BRUSSELS SPROUTS
WITH BACON

Makes 2 servings

Ingredients:

1 pound Brussels sprouts, halved

4 bacon strips, cooked and crumbled

1 tablespoon unsalted butter, melted

2 tablespoons balsamic glaze

A big pinch of chili flakes

Kosher salt and fresh pepper to taste

Method:

1. *Fill the water reservoir with cold water up to the MAX line, fit with drip tray then add steamer basket.*
2. *Place Brussels sprouts into steamer basket and cover.*
3. *Set timer knob to 7 minutes.*
4. *Steam for 7 minutes or until crisp tender.*
5. *When steaming is complete, transfer to a serving bowl.*
6. *Add remaining ingredients, toss to coat then serve hot.*

TIP

If you want to skip the bacon, you can add a 1/4 teaspoon liquid smoke instead.
Liquid smoke can be found near the BBQ sauce section of most grocery stores.

BEEF & BROCCOLI

Makes 2 servings

Ingredients:

8 ounces lean raw beef, thinly sliced

1 garlic clove, chopped

1 coin fresh ginger, chopped

1 tablespoon soy sauce

1 head broccoli, cut into florets

2 tablespoons hoisin sauce, for serving

Sesame seeds, for serving

Method:

1. *Fill the water reservoir with cold water up to the MAX line, fit with drip tray then add steamer basket.*

2. *Combine all ingredients, except hoisin sauce and sesame seeds, in a large plastic zipper top bag then shake to coat.*

3. *Pour zipper top bag contents into steamer basket and cover (use additional steamer baskets if needed).*

4. *Set timer knob to 5 minutes.*

5. *Steam for 5 minutes or until beef is cooked and broccoli is crisp tender.*

6. *When steaming is complete, remove, garnish as desired and serve drizzled with hoisin sauce and sesame seeds.*

TIP

You can use chicken, vegan meat substitute or even tofu instead of the beef for this recipe. You can also use a bag of frozen broccoli instead of using fresh.

BALSAMIC GLAZED
TOFU & KALE

Makes 2 servings

Ingredients:

1 bunch kale, roughly chopped

1/2 small yellow onion, sliced

1 cup grape tomatoes

1 package (1 pound) extra-firm tofu, sliced and drained

Kosher salt and fresh pepper to taste

1/3 cup store-bought balsamic glaze

1/3 cup smoked almonds

Method:

1. *Fill the water reservoir with cold water up to the MAX line, fit with drip tray then add steamer basket.*
2. *Place all ingredients, except salt, pepper, glaze and almonds, into steamer basket and cover (use additional steamer baskets if needed).*
3. *Set timer knob to 8 minutes.*
4. *Steam for 8 minutes or until kale is wilted and tofu is hot.*
5. *When steaming is complete, transfer to a serving bowl.*
6. *Add remaining ingredients and toss to coat.*
7. *Garnish as desired and serve.*

Skinny Steamed
Greens
(See page 17)

COPPER
PENNY SALAD

Makes 4 servings

Ingredients:

1 pound large carrots, cut into thin coins

1/4 cup apple cider vinegar

2 tablespoons canola oil

3 tablespoons honey or other sweetener

2 teaspoons dry mustard

1 teaspoon bottled Worcestershire sauce

1/2 cup ketchup

2 tablespoons sour cream (optional)

Kosher salt and fresh pepper to taste

1/2 small red onion, sliced

Method:

1. *Fill the water reservoir with cold water up to the MAX line, fit with drip tray then add steamer basket.*

2. *Place carrots into steamer basket and cover.*

3. *Set timer knob to 8 minutes.*

4. *Steam for 8 minutes or until carrots are tender.*

5. *When steaming is complete, transfer to a serving bowl.*

6. *Stir in remaining ingredients until combined.*

7. *Garnish as desired and serve.*

STEAMED ARTICHOKES

Makes 2 servings

Ingredients:

For the Artichokes:

2 large artichokes, trimmed

1 lemon, sliced into rounds

For the Dipping Sauce:

1/3 cup mayonnaise or yogurt

1/4 teaspoon fresh lemon zest

1 tablespoon fresh lemon juice

1 teaspoon bottled Worcestershire sauce

1 tablespoon chives, minced

Method:

1. *Fill the water reservoir with cold water up to the MAX line, fit with drip tray then add steamer basket.*
2. *Place artichokes and lemon slices into steamer basket and cover.*
3. *Set timer knob to 30 minutes.*
4. *Steam for 30 minutes or until tender and leaves pull off easily.*
5. *While steaming, whisk together all dipping sauce ingredients in a bowl; set aside.*
6. *When steaming is complete, remove and serve with dipping sauce.*

TIP

If you find baby artichokes at your market, you can skip the trimming and reduce steaming time to 15 minutes or until tender.

MINI STRAWBERRY CHEESECAKE

Makes 2 servings

Ingredients:

2 vanilla wafer cookies

2 large strawberries, stemmed

1 package (8 ounces) cream cheese, softened

2 tablespoons granulated sugar

2 large egg yolks

Additional fresh berries, for serving

Method:

1. Apply nonstick cooking spray to two ramekins or silicone baking cups.
2. Drop a vanilla wafer into the bottom of each ramekin, flat-side down; set aside.
3. In a food processor, combine strawberries, cream cheese and sugar; puree until smooth.
4. Add egg yolks then pulse until just combined.
5. Divide mixture between the ramekins, filling each almost to the top.
6. Fill the water reservoir with cold water up to the MAX line, fit with drip tray then add steamer basket.
7. Place ramekins into steamer basket and cover.
8. Set timer knob to 18 minutes.
9. Steam for 18 minutes or until centers are wobbly when tapped.
10. When steaming is complete, remove, garnish with additional berries and serve warm or cold.

OLD FASHIONED
RICE PUDDING

Makes 2 servings

Ingredients:

1/4 cup granulated sugar

3/4 cup milk

2 tablespoons heavy cream

1/2 teaspoon vanilla extract

Pinch of ground cinnamon

Pinch of kosher salt

1 cup white or brown rice, cooked

Method:

1. *Combine all ingredients in a mixing bowl.*
2. *Divide mixture between 2 ramekins.*
3. *Fill the water reservoir with cold water up to the MAX line, fit with drip tray then add steamer basket.*
4. *Place ramekins into steamer basket and cover.*
5. *Set timer knob to 10 minutes.*
6. *Steam for 10 minutes or until heated through.*
7. *When steaming is complete, remove, garnish as desired and serve.*

TIP

If you prefer thicker rice pudding, let it rest for a few minutes as rice pudding is runny when first made and thickens as it cools.

PECAN TOPPED ACORN SQUASH

Makes 2 servings

Ingredients:

Kosher salt and fresh pepper to taste

1 tablespoon light brown sugar or other sweetener

2 tablespoons pecans, chopped

A few fresh sage leaves

1 acorn squash, cut into rings

Method:

1. *Fill the water reservoir with cold water up to the MAX line, fit with drip tray then add steamer basket.*
2. *Scatter salt, pepper, sugar, pecans and sage over squash rings.*
3. *Place squash into steamer basket and cover (use additional steamer baskets if needed).*
4. *Set timer knob to 15 minutes.*
5. *Steam for 15 minutes or until squash is tender.*
6. *When steaming is complete, remove, garnish as desired and serve.*

SEA BASS &
SPAGHETTI SQUASH

Makes 2 servings

Ingredients:

1 tablespoon mayonnaise or yogurt

1 garlic clove, chopped

1 green onion, sliced

1/2 teaspoon fresh thyme leaves

Kosher salt and fresh pepper to taste

1 small spaghetti squash, halved

2 sea bass fillets or other firm fish

4 cups baby spinach

Method:

1. *Fill the water reservoir with cold water up to the MAX line, fit with drip tray then add 3 steamer baskets.*

2. *In a small bowl, stir together the mayonnaise, garlic, green onions, thyme, salt and pepper; set aside.*

3. *Season squash with salt and pepper.*

4. *Place squash into one steamer basket, cover and set timer knob to 25 minutes.*

5. *Steam for 25 minutes or until cooked through and tender.*

6. *Place fish into second steamer basket, cover and set timer knob to 5 minutes after squash has been steaming for 20 minutes.*

7. *Steam fish for 5 minutes or until just cooked through.*

8. *Place spinach into third steamer basket, cover and set timer knob to 2 minutes after starting to steam the fish.*

9. *Steam for 2 minutes or until wilted.*

10. *When steaming is complete, transfer all to serving plates then scrape squash using a fork to make strands.*

11. *Serve with prepared mayonnaise sauce.*

CHICKEN WITH
PEANUT SAUCE

Makes 2-4 servings

Ingredients:

For the Chicken:

2 raw boneless, skinless chicken thighs or breasts, cubed

Kosher salt and fresh pepper to taste

2 tablespoons fresh cilantro, chopped

For the Peanut Dipping Sauce:

2 garlic cloves, minced

3 tablespoons peanut butter, melted in microwave

2 teaspoons light brown sugar

1 teaspoon bottled sriracha or hot sauce

1 tablespoon tomato paste

2 tablespoons chicken stock

2 tablespoons hoisin sauce

2 tablespoons peanuts, chopped

Method:

1. *Fill the water reservoir with cold water up to the MAX line, fit with drip tray then add steamer basket.*
2. *Season chicken with salt and pepper then place into steamer basket and cover.*
3. *Set timer knob to 8 minutes.*
4. *Steam for 8 minutes or until chicken is cooked through.*
5. *While steaming, whisk together all sauce ingredients in a small bowl then set aside.*
6. *When steaming is complete, remove chicken then sprinkle with cilantro.*
7. *Garnish as desired and serve with skewers and peanut dipping sauce.*

TIP

If you are allergic to peanuts, substitute the peanut butter in the sauce recipe for another nut butter of your choice and skip the chopped peanuts.

RHUBARB COOKIE CRUNCH

Makes 2 servings

Ingredients:

1 1/2 cups fresh or frozen rhubarb, sliced

1/4 cup granulated sugar or other sweetener

1/4 cup shortbread cookies, crumbled

1 tablespoon unsalted butter, melted

Method:

1. *In a bowl, toss together the rhubarb and sugar.*
2. *Divide rhubarb mixture between 2 ramekins.*
3. *Fill the water reservoir with cold water up to the MAX line, fit with drip tray then add steamer basket.*
4. *Place ramekins into steamer basket and cover.*
5. *Set timer knob to 18 minutes.*
6. *Steam for 18 minutes or until rhubarb is soft.*
7. *When steaming is complete, remove and top with cookie crumbs.*
8. *Drizzle with butter, garnish as desired and serve.*

EASY STEAMED
CORNBREAD MINIS

Makes 6 servings

Ingredients:

2 large eggs

2 1/4 cups yellow cornmeal

1/3 cup unsalted butter, melted

1 tablespoon honey or other sweetener

1 teaspoon baking soda

1 teaspoon baking powder

1 teaspoon kosher salt

Method:

1. *Apply nonstick cooking spray to 6 mini loaf pans, ramekins or silicone molds.*
2. *In a mixing bowl, whisk together all ingredients until just smooth.*
3. *Pour batter into pans until each is 2/3 full.*
4. *Fill the water reservoir with cold water up to the MAX line, fit with drip tray then add 3 steamer baskets.*
5. *Place 2 pans into each steamer basket and cover.*
6. *Set timer knobs to 15 minutes.*
7. *Steam for 15 minutes or until tops are firm to the touch.*
8. *When steaming is complete, remove, garnish as desired and serve.*

KITCHEN SINK
MUFFINS

Makes 2 servings with extra batter

Ingredients:

2 large eggs

1/3 cup canola oil

1 teaspoon vanilla extract

1 cup all purpose flour

1/2 cup light brown sugar or other sweetener

1 teaspoon baking soda

1 teaspoon ground all spice

1/2 teaspoon kosher salt

1/2 cup dark raisins

1 cup carrots, grated

1 cup apples, grated

1/2 cup coconut flakes

1/2 cup pecans, chopped

Method:

1. *Apply nonstick cooking spray to 2 ramekins then set aside.*
2. *In a large bowl, whisk together all ingredients until just combined.*
3. *Spoon batter into each prepared ramekin until 2/3 full (you will have extra batter).*
4. *Fill the water reservoir with cold water up to the MAX line, fit with drip tray then add steamer basket.*
5. *Place ramekins into steamer basket and cover.*
6. *Set timer knob to 18 minutes.*
7. *Steam for 18 minutes or until a wooden pick inserted off-center comes out with just a few moist crumbs clinging to it.*
8. *When steaming is complete, remove carefully and serve warm.*

TIP

The batter for these muffins keeps very well for up to 5 days in the refrigerator or up to 3 months in the freezer.

44

STEAK SALAD

Makes 2 servings

Ingredients:

2 sirloin steaks, 4-5 ounces each

Kosher salt and fresh pepper to taste

2 tablespoons soy sauce

2 garlic cloves, chopped

8 cups baby spinach

1/2 cup grape tomatoes, halved

1 small red onion, sliced very thin

2 ounces blue cheese, crumbled

2 ounces walnuts, toasted and chopped

1 ripe pear, diced

Vinaigrette dressing of your choice

Method:

1. *Fill the water reservoir with cold water up to the MAX line, fit with drip tray then add steamer basket.*
2. *Season steaks with salt, pepper, soy sauce and garlic.*
3. *Place steaks into steamer basket and cover.*
4. *Set timer knob to 10 minutes.*
5. *Start checking for desired doneness after about 5 minutes of steaming until desired temperature is achieved.*
6. *When steaming is complete, remove, let cool for 5 minutes then slice thinly.*
7. *In a large bowl, toss steak together with remaining ingredients.*
8. *Garnish as desired and serve.*

SIMPLE STEAMED POTATOES

Makes 3-4 servings

Ingredients:

1 1/2 pounds small potatoes, quartered

Method:

1. *Fill the water reservoir with cold water up to the MAX line, fit with drip tray then add steamer basket.*
2. *Place potatoes into steamer basket and cover (use additional steamer baskets if needed).*
3. *Set timer knob to 15 minutes.*
4. *Steam for 15 minutes or until potatoes are tender.*
5. *When steaming is complete, remove, garnish as desired and serve.*

TIP

To make "dirty mashed potatoes" which are mashed potatoes with skin on, use a potato masher after steaming then add salt, milk and a bit of butter until desired texture is achieved.

MINI BLUEBERRY
UPSIDE DOWN CAKE

Makes 1 cake

Ingredients:

3 tablespoons fresh or frozen blueberries

2 tablespoons whole milk

1 large egg

3 tablespoons vegetable oil

1/4 teaspoon vanilla extract

4 tablespoons all purpose flour

4 tablespoons granulated sugar

Pinch of kosher salt

Method:

1. *Apply nonstick cooking spray to a silicone mold or ramekin then add blueberries; set aside.*
2. *In a small bowl, stir together remaining ingredients using a fork until blended.*
3. *Pour batter over the blueberries inside the silicone mold.*
4. *Fill the water reservoir with cold water up to the MAX line, fit with drip tray then add steamer basket.*
5. *Place silicone mold into steamer basket and cover.*
6. *Set timer knob to 12 minutes.*
7. *Steam for 12 minutes or until cake is firm to the touch.*
8. *When steaming is complete, remove and invert onto a serving dish.*
9. *Garnish as desired and serve.*

TIP

Because the cake part of this recipe is vanilla and pairs well with many flavors, you can get creative and use other fruits or berries as well as chocolate chips or caramel chips in step 1 of this recipe.

FLORIDA
SHRIMP SALAD

Makes 4 servings

Ingredients:

1 pound small shrimp (31-35 count), peeled and deveined

1/2 cup plain yogurt or mayonnaise

1/4 small red onion, chopped

2 green onions, chopped + more for serving

1 celery stalk, diced

2 tablespoons sweet pickle relish

Kosher salt and fresh pepper to taste

Method:

1. *Fill the water reservoir with cold water up to the MAX line, fit with drip tray then add steamer basket.*
2. *Place shrimp into steamer basket and cover.*
3. *Set timer knob to 3 minutes.*
4. *Steam for 3 minutes or until just cooked through and pink.*
5. *When steaming is complete, transfer to a mixing bowl and let cool for 5 minutes.*
6. *Add remaining ingredients and stir to combine.*
7. *Top with additional green onions, garnish as desired and serve cold.*

PASTA WITH CHICKEN &
BROCCOLI

Makes 1 serving

Ingredients:

1/4 cup broccoli florets

1 cup leftover pasta

1 cup leftover rotisserie chicken

1 garlic clove, chopped

1/4 cup chicken stock

Kosher salt and fresh pepper to taste

2 tablespoons Parmesan cheese, grated

2 tablespoons Cheddar cheese, shredded

Method:

1. *Fill the water reservoir with cold water up to the MAX line, fit with drip tray then add steamer basket.*
2. *Place all ingredients into the rice bowl and stir.*
3. *Place rice bowl into steamer basket and cover.*
4. *Set timer knob to 12 minutes.*
5. *Steam for 12 minutes or until heated through and cheese is melted.*
6. *When steaming is complete, remove, garnish as desired and serve.*

MAPLE GLAZED
SWEET POTATOES

Makes 3 servings

Ingredients:

3 small sweet potatoes

Kosher salt and fresh pepper to taste

Fresh parsley, for serving

1 tablespoon unsalted butter, for serving

3 tablespoons maple syrup, for serving

Method:

1. *Fill the water reservoir with cold water up to the MAX line, fit with drip tray then add steamer basket.*
2. *Place sweet potatoes into steamer basket and cover.*
3. *Set timer knob to 30 minutes.*
4. *Steam for 30 minutes or until soft when squeezed.*
5. *When steaming is complete, transfer to a serving plate.*
6. *Season with salt and pepper, top with parsley then serve with butter and maple syrup.*

TIP

You can turn these potatoes into a complete meal by skipping the maple syrup and topping the potatoes with prepared chili, leftover meats or broccoli.

RECIPES

PARTY
BRIE CHEESE

Makes 6 servings

Ingredients:

1 small Brie cheese

1/4 cup store-bought raspberry jam

1/4 cup pecans, toasted and chopped

Crackers or French bread, for dipping

TIP

To find the correct size Brie to fit into the steamer basket, look for the word "petite" on the package of the Brie as it is commonly used to describe a small Brie. Most Brie sold at club stores are too large to fit the steamer basket.

Method:

1. *Fill the water reservoir with cold water up to the MAX line, fit with drip tray then add steamer basket.*
2. *Apply nonstick cooking spray to the bottom of the steamer basket.*
3. *Place the cheese into the steamer basket.*
4. *Top cheese with jam, keeping jam away from the cheese edges.*
5. *Top with the pecans and cover.*
6. *Set timer knob to 6 minutes.*
7. *Steam for 6 minutes or until cheese is soft to the touch.*
8. *When steaming is complete, remove, garnish as desired and serve with crackers or bread.*

LEMON
ASPARAGUS

Makes 4 servings

Ingredients:

1 pound asparagus spears, trimmed or peeled if large

1 teaspoon fresh lemon zest

1 tablespoon fresh lemon juice

1 teaspoon Dijon mustard

1 tablespoon olive oil

Kosher salt and fresh pepper to taste

Method:

1. *Fill the water reservoir with cold water up to the MAX line, fit with drip tray then add steamer basket.*
2. *Place asparagus into steamer basket and cover (use additional steamer baskets if needed).*
3. *Set timer knob to 4 minutes.*
4. *Steam for 4 minutes or until crisp tender.*
5. *When steaming is complete, transfer to a serving plate.*
6. *To make the vinaigrette, whisk together remaining ingredients in a bowl.*
7. *Drizzle vinaigrette over asparagus before serving.*

COCONUT RICE

Makes 2-4 servings

Ingredients:

1 cup basmati rice, rinsed

1/2 cup coconut milk

Kosher salt to taste (optional)

1 3/4 cups boiling water

1/4 cup coconut flakes

2 green onions, chopped

Method:

1. *Fill the water reservoir with cold water up to the MAX line, fit with drip tray then add steamer basket.*
2. *Place rice, coconut milk, salt and water into the rice bowl and stir.*
3. *Place rice bowl into steamer basket and cover.*
4. *Set timer knob to 30 minutes.*
5. *Steam for 30 minutes or until rice is tender.*
6. *When steaming is complete, transfer rice to a serving bowl.*
7. *Stir in remaining ingredients before serving.*

CRANBERRY TURKEY
TENDERLOIN

Makes 2 servings

Ingredients:

1 small turkey tenderloin, raw

Kosher salt and fresh pepper to taste

1/2 teaspoon dried sage

1/2 cup cranberry relish or sauce, for serving

Method:

1. *Fill the water reservoir with cold water up to the MAX line, fit with drip tray then add steamer basket.*
2. *Season turkey with salt, pepper and sage.*
3. *Place turkey into steamer basket and cover.*
4. *Set timer knob to 20 minutes.*
5. *Steam for 20 minutes or until cooked through.*
6. *When steaming is complete, remove, garnish as desired and serve with cranberry relish.*

STEAMED CABBAGE WITH BUTTER

Makes 2 servings

Ingredients:

1/4 small head cabbage, cut into wedges

2 teaspoons unsalted butter

Kosher salt and fresh pepper to taste

Method:

1. Fill the water reservoir with cold water up to the MAX line, fit with drip tray then add steamer basket.
2. Place cabbage into steamer basket and cover.
3. Set timer knob to 8 minutes.
4. Steam for 8 minutes or until cabbage is crisp tender.
5. When steaming is complete, transfer to a serving bowl.
6. Top with butter then season with salt and pepper before serving.

CRUNCHY BANANA
PECAN CUPS

Makes 2 servings

Ingredients:

2 small bananas

1/2 of a lemon

2 tablespoons jarred caramel sauce

Pinch of kosher salt

1/4 teaspoon vanilla extract

1 tablespoon banana liqueur (optional)

2 teaspoons unsalted butter, melted

1/4 cup pecans, toasted

Method:

1. *Slice bananas into 2 ramekins.*
2. *Squeeze some lemon juice over the bananas in each ramekin.*
3. *In a small bowl, stir together the caramel, salt, vanilla, liqueur and butter.*
4. *Divide this mixture between the ramekins and pour over bananas.*
5. *Fill the water reservoir with cold water up to the MAX line, fit with drip tray then add steamer basket.*
6. *Place ramekins into steamer basket and cover.*
7. *Set timer knob to 10 minutes.*
8. *Steam for 10 minutes or until hot.*
9. *When steaming is complete, remove then top with pecans.*
10. *Garnish as desired and serve.*

TIP

It is normal for the bananas to take on a pinkish hue from steaming.

SALTED CARAMEL CUPS

Makes 2 servings

Ingredients:

1/4 cup canned Dulce de Leche

Pinch of kosher salt + more for serving

2 tablespoons unsalted butter, melted

1/2 teaspoon vanilla extract

1/2 cup heavy cream

4 large egg yolks

Method:

1. *Apply nonstick cooking spray to 2 ramekins or mini bowls.*
2. *In a mixing bowl, whisk together all ingredients until smooth.*
3. *Divide mixture between the prepared ramekins.*
4. *Fill the water reservoir with cold water up to the MAX line, fit with drip tray then add steamer basket.*
5. *Place ramekins into steamer basket and cover.*
6. *Set timer knob to 18 minutes.*
7. *Steam for 18 minutes or until wobbly in center when tapped.*
8. *Sprinkle with additional salt, garnish as desired and serve warm or cold.*

SKINNY STEAMED BUFFALO WINGS

Makes 2 servings

Ingredients:

12 chicken wings, flats and drumettes, raw

Kosher salt and fresh pepper to taste

Bottled wing sauce

Blue cheese and celery, for serving

Method:

1. *Fill the water reservoir with cold water up to the MAX line, fit with drip tray then add steamer basket.*
2. *Season wings with salt and pepper.*
3. *Place wings into steamer basket and cover (use additional steamer baskets if needed).*
4. *Set timer knob to 20 minutes.*
5. *Steam for 20 minutes or until wings are cooked through.*
6. *When steaming is complete, transfer to a bowl then toss with wing sauce.*
7. *Serve with blue cheese and celery.*

TIP

For crispier wings, transfer to a sheet pan after steaming then place under the broiler for 2-3 minutes. If you don't like chicken with bones, use chicken breast strips or tenders instead then steam for 8-10 minutes or until cooked through.

SPICY YELLOW SQUASH & TOMATOES

Makes 4 servings

Ingredients:

3 large yellow squashes, sliced

1 small yellow onion, sliced

1 cup grape tomatoes

1 tablespoon extra-virgin olive oil

2 teaspoons apple cider vinegar

1 teaspoon honey

A big pinch of chili flakes

1 garlic clove, minced

Kosher salt and fresh pepper to taste

Method:

1. *Fill the water reservoir with cold water up to the MAX line, fit with drip tray then add steamer basket.*
2. *Place squashes, onions and tomatoes into steamer basket and cover (use additional steamer baskets if needed).*
3. *Set timer knob to 6 minutes.*
4. *Steam for 6 minutes or until squashes are translucent and tomatoes are beginning to split.*
5. *When steaming is complete, transfer all to a serving bowl.*
6. *Stir in remaining ingredients, garnish as desired and serve.*

CHINESE BOK CHOY

Makes 2 servings

Ingredients:

3 baby bok choy, split lengthwise

2 tablespoons bottled Asian sesame dressing, for serving

1 teaspoon sesame seeds, for serving (optional)

Method:

1. *Fill the water reservoir with cold water up to the MAX line, fit with drip tray then add steamer basket.*
2. *Place bok choy into steamer basket and cover.*
3. *Set timer knob to 5 minutes.*
4. *Steam for 5 minutes or until crisp tender.*
5. *When steaming is complete, remove, drizzle with dressing then sprinkle with sesame seeds if desired before serving.*

CHICKEN & APPLE
SALAD

Makes 2 servings

Ingredients:

2 boneless, skinless chicken breasts, raw

1/2 celery stalk, diced

1/4 medium red onion, diced

1/4 Golden Delicious apple, diced

1 tablespoon raisins

1/4 cup red seedless grapes, halved

1 tablespoon sweet pickle relish

1/4 cup mayonnaise or yogurt

1 teaspoon yellow mustard

Kosher salt and fresh pepper to taste

Sandwich bread, for serving (optional)

Method:

1. *Fill the water reservoir with cold water up to the MAX line, fit with drip tray then add steamer basket.*
2. *Place chicken into steamer basket and cover.*
3. *Set timer knob to 12 minutes.*
4. *Steam for 12 minutes or until chicken is cooked through.*
5. *When steaming is complete, remove to a bowl and let cool for 15 minutes.*
6. *Chop or dice the chicken then stir in remaining ingredients, except bread.*
7. *Serve on bread or use as desired.*

SPICY STEAMED COD

Makes 2 servings

Ingredients:

2 cod fillets, minimum 1-inch thick

1 tablespoon bottled soy sauce

2 teaspoons honey

1 red or green jalapeño pepper, sliced

2 teaspoons bottled sriracha or other hot sauce

1 green onion, thinly sliced

Method:

1. *Fill the water reservoir with cold water up to the MAX line, fit with drip tray then add steamer basket.*
2. *Place all ingredients into a plastic zipper top bag then toss gently until fish is coated.*
3. *Transfer bag contents to the steamer basket and cover.*
4. *Set timer knob to 5 minutes.*
5. *Steam for 5 minutes or until fish is just cooked through.*
6. *When steaming is complete, remove, garnish as desired and serve.*

SWEET POTATOES WITH MARSHMALLOWS

Makes 2 servings

Ingredients:

2 large sweet potatoes

4 teaspoons unsalted butter

Kosher salt to taste

4 teaspoons maple syrup

1 cup mini marshmallows

Ground cinnamon, for sprinkling

Method:

1. *Slice sweet potatoes in half lengthwise.*
2. *Fill the water reservoir with cold water up to the MAX line, fit with drip tray then add steamer basket.*
3. *Place potatoes into steamer basket and cover (use additional steamer baskets if needed).*
4. *Set timer knob to 18 minutes.*
5. *Steam for 18 minutes or until just cooked through.*
6. *Remove potatoes then poke holes all over the cut surface of the potatoes using a fork.*
7. *Spread a teaspoon of butter over each potato half then season with salt and drizzle with maple syrup.*
8. *Top with marshmallows, sprinkle with cinnamon then return to steamer.*
9. *Reset timer knob and steam for an additional 1-2 minutes or just until marshmallows begin to melt.*
10. *When steaming is complete, carefully remove using a spatula.*
11. *Garnish as desired and serve hot.*

TIP

For a nice crunch, add a layer of chopped pecans under the marshmallows then place under the broiler for 1-2 minutes until marshmallows are puffed and browned.

EGGS IN A JAR

Makes 4 servings

Ingredients:

4 large eggs

1/3 cup cottage cheese

1/4 cup Parmesan cheese, grated

1/4 cup ham, diced

Kosher salt and fresh pepper to taste

Method:

1. *Place all ingredients into a mixing bowl then whisk until smooth.*
2. *Pour mixture into four 4-ounce size canning jars then add lids.*
3. *Fill the water reservoir with cold water up to the MAX line, fit with drip tray then add steamer basket.*
4. *Place jars into steamer basket and cover (use additional steamer baskets if needed).*
5. *Set timer knob to 12 minutes.*
6. *Steam for 12 minutes or until eggs are set.*
7. *When steaming is complete, remove, garnish as desired and serve.*

TIP

Eggs in a Jar can be made several days ahead for a simple on-the-go breakfast. They are also great using only egg whites.

MASHED
SWEET POTATOES

Makes 2 servings

Ingredients:

1 pound sweet potatoes, peeled and cut into 1-inch chunks

2 tablespoons unsalted butter

1 tablespoon maple syrup or honey

2 tablespoons whole milk or half & half

Kosher salt to taste

Method:

1. *Fill the water reservoir with cold water up to the MAX line, fit with drip tray then add steamer basket.*
2. *Place potatoes into steamer basket and cover.*
3. *Set timer knob to 10 minutes.*
4. *Steam for 10 minutes or until potatoes are tender.*
5. *When steaming is complete, transfer potatoes to a food processor.*
6. *Add remaining ingredients to food processor, cover and pulse until smooth.*
7. *Garnish as desired and serve.*

TIP

If you don't have a food processor, you can mash the potatoes using a fork.

STEAMED BOSTON BROWN BREAD

Makes 2 small breads

Ingredients:

1/4 cup unbleached all purpose flour

1/2 cup 100% whole wheat flour

1/4 cup rye flour

1/2 cup yellow cornmeal

1 teaspoon ground cinnamon

1/2 teaspoon kosher salt

1/2 teaspoon baking soda

1 cup buttermilk

1/3 cup molasses

1/2 cup dark raisins

Kosher salt and butter, for serving

Method:

1. *Apply nonstick cooking spray to 2 clean soup cans.*
2. *In a large mixing bowl, whisk together the flours, cornmeal, cinnamon, salt and baking soda using a hand whisk.*
3. *Whisk in the buttermilk, molasses and raisins.*
4. *Spoon batter into each soup can until 3/4 full.*
5. *Tightly cover cans with small squares of nonstick aluminum foil.*
6. *Fill the water reservoir with cold water up to the MAX line, fit with drip tray then add steamer basket.*
7. *Place cans into steamer basket and cover.*
8. *Set timer knob to 25 minutes.*
9. *When steaming is complete, use a wooden pick to test for doneness, it should come out with just a few moist crumbs clinging to it. If it is not done, keep steaming in 5-minute increments until done.*
10. *Remove cans and let cool for 10 minutes before serving.*
11. *Serve bread with salt and butter.*

TIP

This very old classic recipe is traditionally steamed in cans. However, you can use any type of vessel such as ramekins, silicone molds or coffee cups that fit inside the steamer baskets.

MASHED POTATOES

Makes 4 servings

Ingredients:

3 pounds Russet or Yukon gold potatoes, peeled and quartered

3 tablespoons unsalted butter

Kosher salt to taste

1 cup or more whole milk or half & half

Chopped parsley, for serving

Method:

1. *Fill the water reservoir with cold water up to the MAX line, fit with drip tray then add steamer basket.*
2. *Place potatoes into steamer basket and cover (use additional steamer baskets if needed).*
3. *Set timer knob to 20 minutes.*
4. *Steam for 20 minutes or until potatoes are tender.*
5. *When steaming is complete, transfer potatoes to a bowl.*
6. *Add the butter and a bit of salt then mash using a potato masher.*
7. *Add the milk in stages until desired texture is achieved.*
8. *Garnish with parsley before serving.*

TIP

Some of my favorite add-ins to mashed potatoes are goat cheese, pesto or even store-bought tapenade. For lighter mashed potatoes, I use a little bit of olive oil and buttermilk instead of milk.

Carrots with Cilantro & Lime
(See page 94)

CILANTRO RICE

Makes 2-4 servings

Ingredients:

1 cup basmati rice, uncooked

1 tablespoon vegetable oil

2 cups boiling water

1 teaspoon lime zest

2 tablespoons fresh lime juice

1 bunch cilantro, pureed + chopped cilantro for serving

Kosher salt to taste

Method:

1. *Fill the water reservoir with cold water up to the MAX line, fit with drip tray then add steamer basket.*
2. *Place rice, oil and water into the rice bowl and stir.*
3. *Place rice bowl into steamer basket and cover.*
4. *Set timer knob to 30 minutes.*
5. *Steam for 30 minutes or until rice is tender.*
6. *When steaming is complete, transfer rice to a serving bowl.*
7. *Stir in remaining ingredients.*
8. *Garnish as desired and serve.*

STEAMED HALIBUT & SNOW PEAS

Makes 2 servings

Ingredients:

1 small purple onion, sliced

2 halibut fillets or other firm white fish

Kosher salt and fresh pepper to taste

2 cups snow peas

2 cups grape tomatoes

Method:

1. *Fill the water reservoir with cold water up to the MAX line, fit with drip tray then add 3 steamer baskets.*

2. *Place onions into one steamer basket, top with fish then season with salt and pepper; cover then set timer knob to 5 minutes and steam until fish is just cooked through.*

3. *Place snow peas into second steamer basket, cover and set timer knob to 3 minutes.*

4. *Place tomatoes into third steamer basket, cover and set timer knob to 2 minutes.*

5. *When steaming is complete, remove, garnish as desired and serve.*

RECIPES

HONEY JALAPEÑO MEATBALLS

Makes 2 servings

Ingredients:

1 pound ground chicken

1 large egg

2 tablespoons whole milk

1 bread slice, torn into pieces

Kosher salt and fresh pepper to taste

2 green onions, chopped

2 garlic cloves, chopped

1 jalapeño pepper, diced

3 tablespoons honey + more for serving

Method:

1. *Combine all ingredients in a mixing bowl.*
2. *Shape mixture into 8 meatballs.*
3. *Fill the water reservoir with cold water up to the MAX line, fit with drip tray then add steamer basket.*
4. *Place meatballs into steamer basket and cover.*
5. *Set timer knob to 10 minutes.*
6. *Steam for 10 minutes or until meatballs are cooked through.*
7. *When steaming is complete, remove, drizzle with additional honey, garnish as desired and serve.*

STEAMED RICE

Makes 2 servings

Ingredients:

1/2 cup long grain white rice, such as basmati, uncooked

1 cup boiling water

Method:

1. Fill the water reservoir with cold water up to the MAX line, fit with drip tray then add steamer basket.
2. Place all ingredients into rice bowl and stir.
3. Place rice bowl into steamer basket and cover.
4. Set timer knob to 30 minutes.
5. Steam for 30 minutes or until rice is tender.
6. When steaming is complete, transfer rice to a bowl.
7. Fluff rice using a fork, garnish as desired and serve.

STEAMED PEACH BREAD PUDDING

Makes 2 servings

Ingredients:

2 large eggs

1/3 cup whole milk

A pinch of kosher salt

1 teaspoon lemon juice

3 tablespoons granulated sugar or other sweetener

1 cup frozen peach slices

1 bread slice, torn

Method:

1. *In a mixing bowl, whisk together the eggs, milk, salt, lemon juice and sugar.*
2. *Fold in remaining ingredients then divide between 2 mini dishes or silicone molds.*
3. *Fill the water reservoir with cold water up to the MAX line, fit with drip tray then add steamer basket.*
4. *Place mini dishes into steamer basket and cover.*
5. *Set timer knob to 18 minutes.*
6. *Steam for 18 minutes or until firm to the touch.*
7. *When steaming is complete, remove, garnish as desired and serve.*

STEAMED PEARS

Makes 2 servings

Ingredients:

2 ripe pears

1 teaspoon fresh lemon juice

2 tablespoons granulated sugar or other sweetener

3 tablespoons pecans, toasted and chopped

Method:

1. *Using a melon baller, remove the core and seeds from each pear without piercing the bottom of each pear.*
2. *In a small bowl, stir together remaining ingredients.*
3. *Fill each pear cavity with pecan mixture.*
4. *Fill the water reservoir with cold water up to the MAX line, fit with drip tray then add steamer basket.*
5. *Place pears into steamer basket and cover.*
6. *Set timer knob to 15 minutes.*
7. *Steam for 15 minutes or until pears are soft when squeezed with a towel.*
8. *When steaming is complete, remove carefully as the center will be hot and liquid.*
9. *Garnish as desired and serve warm.*

TIP

If you don't have a melon baller, you can use the teaspoon size from a measuring spoon set. It has the same shape as a melon baller and fits nicely inside the pears.

ZUCCHINI & TOMATOES

Makes 4 servings

Ingredients:

3 zucchini, sliced

1 small yellow onion, sliced

2 cups grape tomatoes

1 tablespoon unsalted butter

Kosher salt and fresh pepper to taste

Method:

1. *Fill the water reservoir with cold water up to the MAX line, fit with drip tray then add steamer basket.*
2. *Place zucchini, onions and tomatoes into steamer basket and cover (use additional steamer baskets if needed).*
3. *Set timer knob to 6 minutes.*
4. *Steam for 6 minutes or until zucchini is translucent and tomatoes are beginning to split.*
5. *When steaming is complete, transfer to a serving bowl.*
6. *Stir in remaining ingredients, garnish as desired and serve.*

VEGETARIAN
STUFFED PEPPERS

Makes 2 servings

Ingredients:

1 cup rice, cooked

1/2 cup tomato, finely chopped

1 small yellow onion, finely chopped

1 tablespoon olive oil

Kosher salt and fresh pepper to taste

1/3 cup Parmesan cheese, grated

2 large bell peppers, tops reserved

Method:

1. *In a mixing bowl, combine all ingredients, except bell peppers.*
2. *Trim the bottom of each bell pepper without making a hole so they sit flat then remove core.*
3. *Divide rice mixture between the bell peppers then cover peppers with reserved tops.*
4. *Fill the water reservoir with cold water up to the MAX line, fit with drip tray then add steamer basket.*
5. *Place peppers into steamer basket and cover.*
6. *Set timer knob to 18 minutes.*
7. *Steam for 18 minutes or until peppers are tender.*
8. *When steaming is complete, remove, garnish as desired and serve.*

TIP

If you accidentally cut a hole into the bottom of the peppers, use the trimmed off scraps from step 2 to patch the hole.

FOOLPROOF
POACHED EGGS

Makes 2 servings

Ingredients:

2 large eggs
Kosher salt and fresh pepper to taste

Method:

1. *Apply nonstick cooking spray to 2 ramekins then crack 1 egg into each ramekin.*
2. *Fill the water reservoir with cold water up to the MAX line, fit with drip tray then add steamer basket.*
3. *Place ramekins into steamer basket and cover.*
4. *Set timer knob to 5 minutes.*
5. *Steam for 5 minutes or until egg white is slightly firm.*
6. *When steaming is complete, carefully remove ramekins.*
7. *Remove eggs from ramekins using a spoon.*
8. *Season to taste with salt and pepper, garnish as desired and serve.*

CAULIFLOWER
MASH

Makes 2 servings

Ingredients:

1 small head cauliflower, cut into florets

1/4 cup plain Greek yogurt

1 tablespoon unsalted butter (optional)

Kosher salt and fresh pepper to taste

Method:

1. *Fill the water reservoir with cold water up to the MAX line, fit with drip tray then add steamer basket.*
2. *Place cauliflower into steamer basket and cover.*
3. *Set timer knob to 7 minutes.*
4. *Steam for 7 minutes or until fork tender.*
5. *When steaming is complete, transfer cauliflower to a food processor fitted with the "S" blade.*
6. *Add remaining ingredients to food processor, cover then process until smooth.*
7. *Garnish as desired and serve.*

TIP

If you don't have a food processor, you can use a potato masher for a somewhat chunkier consistency.

CHINESE-STYLE CHICKEN SALAD

Makes 2 servings

Ingredients:

For the Salad:

2 raw boneless, skinless chicken breasts, cubed

Kosher salt and fresh pepper to taste

2 cups iceberg lettuce, shredded

1 carrot, finely julienned

1 small wedge purple cabbage, sliced

2 green onions, thinly sliced

1/2 cup canned Mandarin orange segments

1/4 cup roasted peanuts, chopped

1/4 cup cilantro leaves

For the Dressing:

3 tablespoons dry mustard

4 tablespoons rice wine vinegar

1/2 cup canola oil

Kosher salt and fresh pepper to taste

3 tablespoons honey

1 tablespoon bottled soy sauce

1 teaspoon dark sesame oil

Method:

1. *Fill the water reservoir with cold water up to the MAX line, fit with drip tray then add steamer basket.*
2. *Season chicken with salt and pepper then place into steamer basket and cover.*
3. *Set timer knob to 8 minutes.*
4. *Steam for 8 minutes or until chicken is cooked through.*
5. *When steaming is complete, transfer chicken to a bowl and let cool for 10 minutes.*
6. *Add remaining salad ingredients to the bowl then toss to combine.*
7. *In a small bowl, whisk together all dressing ingredients.*
8. *Drizzle dressing over salad, garnish as desired and serve.*

STICKY RICE

Makes 2 servings

Ingredients:

1/2 cup short grain rice, uncooked

Method:

1. *Pour rice into the rice bowl.*
2. *Add water to rice bowl until water level exceeds rice by 2-inches.*
3. *Let soak at room temperature for 8 hours.*
4. *Drain the water but keep the rice inside the rice bowl.*
5. *Fill the water reservoir with cold water up to the MAX line, fit with drip tray then add steamer basket.*
6. *Place rice bowl into steamer basket and cover.*
7. *Set timer knob to 20 minutes.*
8. *Steam for 20 minutes or until rice is tender.*
9. *When steaming is complete, transfer rice to a serving bowl.*
10. *Garnish as desired and serve.*

GARLIC CHICKEN THIGHS

Makes 1 serving

Ingredients:

2 chicken thighs, raw

2 garlic cloves, minced

1 green onion, chopped

1/4 teaspoon dried thyme

1 teaspoon olive oil

Kosher salt and fresh pepper to taste

Method:

1. *Fill the water reservoir with cold water up to the MAX line, fit with drip tray then add steamer basket.*
2. *Place all ingredients into the rice bowl and stir.*
3. *Place rice bowl into steamer basket and cover.*
4. *Set timer knob to 20 minutes.*
5. *Steam for 20 minutes or until chicken is cooked through.*
6. *When cooking is complete, remove, garnish as desired and serve.*

DEVILED EGGS

Makes 12 egg halves

Ingredients:

6 large eggs

1/4 cup mayonnaise

1 teaspoon yellow mustard

1 tablespoon sweet pickle relish

1/2 teaspoon kosher salt

Pinch of cayenne pepper

1 teaspoon apple cider vinegar

Paprika, for sprinkling

Method:

1. *Fill the water reservoir with cold water up to the MAX line, fit with drip tray then add steamer basket.*
2. *Place eggs into steamer basket and cover.*
3. *Set timer knob to 12 minutes.*
4. *When steaming is complete, remove eggs then crack shells all over the place in a bowl of cold water.*
5. *Peel eggs under a hard stream of cold water from the faucet then cut in half lengthwise.*
6. *Remove the egg yolks then place the yolks into a bowl and set aside egg white halves.*
7. *Mash the egg yolks using a fork.*
8. *Add remaining ingredients, except paprika, to the egg yolks.*
9. *Mix together using a large spoon then adjust seasoning if desired.*
10. *Transfer egg mixture to a pastry bag or plastic zipper top bag then pipe into the egg white halves.*
11. *Sprinkle with paprika then cover and chill until ready to serve.*

TIP

Deviled eggs have become a very popular restaurant appetizer and are offered in many flavors such as smoked paprika, tuna, capers, smoked salmon and curry. To change the flavor, simply add the desired ingredients in step 8.

CARROTS WITH
CILANTRO & LIME

Makes 2 servings

Ingredients:

1 pound carrots, sliced

1 tablespoon unsalted butter, melted

2 teaspoons fresh lime juice

1 tablespoon fresh cilantro, chopped

Kosher salt and fresh pepper to taste

Method:

1. *Fill the water reservoir with cold water up to the MAX line, fit with drip tray then add steamer basket.*
2. *Place carrots into steamer basket and cover.*
3. *Set timer knob to 10 minutes.*
4. *Steam for 10 minutes or until crisp tender.*
5. *When steaming is complete, transfer carrots to a serving bowl.*
6. *Toss with butter, lime juice, cilantro, salt and pepper.*
7. *Garnish as desired and serve.*

LOBSTER TAILS WITH
HERBED BUTTER

Makes 2 servings

Ingredients:

For the Lobster Tails:

2 lobster tails (8-10 ounces each)

For the Herbed Butter Sauce:

1/4 cup unsalted butter, room temperature

1/4 teaspoon lemon zest

2 teaspoons fresh lemon juice

1 teaspoon fresh dill, finely chopped

1 teaspoon fresh parsley, finely chopped

1 green onion, finely chopped

Kosher salt and fresh pepper to taste

Method:

1. *Fill the water reservoir with cold water up to the MAX line, fit with drip tray then add steamer basket.*
2. *Place lobster tails into steamer basket and cover.*
3. *Set timer knob to 12 minutes.*
4. *Steam for 12 minutes or until just cooked through.*
5. *While lobster tails are steaming, combine all sauce ingredients in a microwave-safe bowl.*
6. *Microwave for 1 minute or until melted.*
7. *When steaming is complete, transfer to dinner plates.*
8. *Serve lobster tails with herbed butter sauce.*

TIP

You can use frozen tails in the steamer as well by adding 8-10 minutes to the total steaming time.

Lemon Asparagus
(See page 58)

SAUERKRAUT &
SAUSAGE

Makes 2 servings

Ingredients:

1 kielbasa sausage link, sliced

4 petite red potatoes, halved

1 carrot, sliced

1/2 small yellow onion, sliced

Kosher salt and fresh pepper to taste

2 cups sauerkraut

1/2 teaspoon caraway seeds (optional)

Fresh parsley, for serving

Method:

1. *Fill the water reservoir with cold water up to the MAX line, fit with drip tray then add 2 steamer baskets.*
2. *Place sausage, potatoes, carrots, onions, salt and pepper into one steamer basket and cover.*
3. *Set timer knob to 12 minutes.*
4. *Steam for 12 minutes or until potatoes are tender.*
5. *Place sauerkraut and caraway seeds into the rice bowl then place into second steamer basket and cover.*
6. *Set timer knob to 12 minutes.*
7. *When steaming is complete, transfer all to a serving platter.*
8. *Sprinkle with parsley before serving.*

TIP

You can use different sausages in this recipe. Many popular sausages include chicken, turkey, venison and even vegan versions. Cooking time does not need to be adjusted as most sausages are already precooked and only require the steaming to be heated through.

STEAMED EDAMAME WITH SMOKED SALT

Makes 2 servings

Ingredients:

1 pound frozen edamame, in the shell

Smoked salt or kosher salt, for serving

Method:

1. *Fill the water reservoir with cold water up to the MAX line, fit with drip tray then add steamer basket.*
2. *Place edamame into steamer basket and cover.*
3. *Set timer knob to 7 minutes.*
4. *Steam for 7 minutes or until edamame are heated through.*
5. *When steaming is complete, transfer to a serving bowl.*
6. *Sprinkle with salt before serving.*

TIP

If you don't have smoked salt, you can use another salt-based seasoning instead.

BROCCOLI WITH CASHEWS & ORANGE

Makes 2 servings

Ingredients:

1 small head broccoli, cut into florets

3 tablespoons cashews, toasted

1/4 cup canned Mandarin orange segments

1 tablespoon soy sauce

1 tablespoon hoisin sauce

Method:

1. *Fill the water reservoir with cold water up to the MAX line, fit with drip tray then add steamer basket.*
2. *Place broccoli into steamer basket and cover.*
3. *Set timer knob to 5 minutes.*
4. *Steam for 5 minutes or until crisp tender.*
5. *When steaming is complete, transfer broccoli to serving plates.*
6. *Top broccoli with cashews, oranges, soy sauce and hoisin sauce before serving.*

Steamed Rice
(See page 80)

CABBAGE ROLLS

Makes 4 servings

Ingredients:

4 large cabbage leaves

For the Meat:

1 pound bulk sage sausage, raw

1/2 yellow onion, chopped

1/2 cup rice, cooked

Kosher salt and fresh pepper to taste

For the Sauce:

1 can (8 ounces) tomato puree

1 teaspoon dry mustard powder

2 tablespoons granulated sugar or other sugar substitute

2 tablespoons apple cider vinegar

Kosher salt or to taste

Method:

1. *Fill the water reservoir with cold water up to the MAX line, fit with drip tray then add steamer basket.*
2. *Place cabbage leaves into steamer basket and cover (use additional steamer baskets if needed).*
3. *Set timer knob to 8 minutes.*
4. *Steam for 8 minutes or until pliable then remove and set aside.*
5. *Mix all meat ingredients together in a small bowl then divide into 4 pieces.*
6. *Place each meat piece into a cabbage leaf then roll up like a burrito.*
7. *Place rolls into steamer baskets, seam-side down, and cover.*
8. *Reset timer knob to 30 minutes.*
9. *Steam for 30 minutes or until cooked through then transfer to serving plates.*
10. *Combine all sauce ingredients in a microwave-safe bowl.*
11. *Heat in microwave for 2-3 minutes or until hot.*
12. *Garnish cabbage rolls as desired and serve with sauce.*

TIP

Cabbage rolls freeze very well. This is a perfect recipe to make a larger batch and freeze for future meals. You can reheat frozen cabbage rolls straight from the freezer by steaming for 15 minutes.

Mashed Potatoes
(See page 76)

RECIPES

APPLE CIDER BRINED
PORK CHOPS

Makes 2 servings

Ingredients:

4 cups apple cider

3 tablespoons kosher salt (or 1 1/2 tablespoons other salt)

2 tablespoons brown sugar

1 tablespoon fresh pepper

2 raw pork chops, 1-inch thick

Method:

1. *In a mixing bowl, combine apple cider, salt, sugar and pepper; whisk until dissolved.*
2. *Place pork chops into the brine then cover with plastic wrap.*
3. *Place bowl in the refrigerator for 2 hours.*
4. *Fill the water reservoir with cold water up to the MAX line, fit with drip tray then add steamer basket.*
5. *Place pork chops into steamer basket and cover (use additional steamer baskets if needed).*
6. *Set timer knob to 10 minutes.*
7. *Steam for 10 minutes or until cooked through.*
8. *When steaming is complete, remove, garnish as desired and serve.*

**Carrots with
Cilantro & Lime**
(See page 94)

**Simple
Steamed Potatoes**
(See page 47)

STEAMED ORANGE CAKE

Makes 1 cake

Ingredients:

2 tablespoons juice from a can of Mandarin oranges

3 tablespoons canned Mandarin orange segments, drained

1 large egg

2 tablespoons vegetable oil

4 tablespoons all purpose flour or cornstarch

3 tablespoons granulated sugar or other sweetener

Pinch of kosher salt

1/4 teaspoon vanilla extract

Method:

1. *Place all ingredients into a mug or ramekin then stir using a fork until blended together.*
2. *Fill the water reservoir with cold water up to the MAX line, fit with drip tray then add steamer basket.*
3. *Place mug into steamer basket and cover.*
4. *Set timer knob to 18 minutes.*
5. *Steam for 18 minutes or until center is firm to the touch.*
6. *When steaming is complete, remove, garnish as desired and serve.*

EASY BEEF
MEATBALLS

Makes 2-4 servings

Ingredients:

1 pound lean ground beef

1/4 cup yellow onions, finely chopped

1/4 cup whole milk

1/2 cup bread crumbs

2 teaspoons unflavored gelatin (optional)

2 teaspoons Italian seasoning

1 teaspoon bottled Worcestershire sauce

Kosher salt and fresh pepper to taste

Method:

1. *Fill the water reservoir with cold water up to the MAX line, fit with drip tray then add steamer basket.*
2. *Stir all ingredients together in a mixing bowl.*
3. *Divide the beef mixture into 8 portions.*
4. *Using your hands, form each portion into a ball.*
5. *Place meatballs into steamer basket and cover.*
6. *Set timer knob to 12 minutes.*
7. *Steam for 12 minutes or until meatballs are cooked through.*
8. *When steaming is complete, remove, garnish as desired and serve.*

TIP

The best way to test for doneness is using a meat thermometer. Meatballs are done at internal temperature of 165°F.

STEAMED
PORK BUNS

Makes 4 servings

Ingredients:

1 large boneless pork country rib

Kosher salt and fresh pepper to taste

8 frozen Bao buns (available at Asian markets)

1 small cucumber, thinly sliced

Hoisin sauce, sliced green onions and rice vinegar, for serving

Method:

1. *Fill the water reservoir with cold water up to the MAX line, fit with drip tray then add steamer basket.*
2. *Season pork with salt and pepper then place into steamer basket and cover.*
3. *Set timer knob to 30 minutes.*
4. *Steam for 30 minutes or until pork is tender.*
5. *When steaming is complete, remove, let cool for 10 minutes then cut into thin slices.*
6. *Steam Bao buns for 1 minute.*
7. *Serve buns with slices of pork and remaining ingredients.*

TIP

There are many different kinds of Bao buns. The ones used in this recipe are called "plain and folded". You can substitute these buns with plain, white sandwich bread with the crusts removed.

POT ROAST

Makes 2 servings

Ingredients:

For the Pot Roast:

8 ounces raw beef chuck roast, sliced

Kosher salt and fresh pepper to taste

1 small yellow onion, chunked

4 small potatoes, halved

1 carrot, sliced

1 small celery stalk, sliced

For the Sauce:

1/2 cup beef stock

1 tablespoon cornstarch

2 tablespoons red wine

Kosher salt and fresh pepper to taste

1 teaspoon onion powder

1 teaspoon paprika

1 bay leaf

Method:

1. *Fill the water reservoir with cold water up to the MAX line, fit with drip tray then add steamer basket.*
2. *Place all pot roast ingredients into steamer basket and cover (use additional steamer baskets if needed).*
3. *Set timer knob to 30 minutes.*
4. *Steam for 30 minutes or until meat is tender.*
5. *When steaming is complete, transfer steamer contents to a serving dish.*
6. *In a microwave-safe bowl, whisk together all sauce ingredients until smooth.*
7. *Heat in microwave for 3-4 minutes or until boiling.*
8. *Pour sauce over meat and vegetables then stir to coat.*
9. *Garnish as desired and serve.*

TIP

It is important to slice the beef thinly. Thick beef pieces might need additional steaming time until tender.

EGG SALAD

Makes 4 servings

Ingredients:

6 large eggs

1/4 cup mayonnaise

1 teaspoon yellow mustard

1 tablespoon sweet pickle relish

2 tablespoons yellow onion, finely chopped

Kosher salt and fresh pepper to taste

Pinch of cayenne pepper

1 teaspoon cider vinegar

Method:

1. *Fill the water reservoir with cold water up to the MAX line, fit with drip tray then add steamer basket.*
2. *Place eggs into steamer basket and cover.*
3. *Set timer knob to 12 minutes.*
4. *When steaming is complete, remove eggs then crack shells all over.*
5. *Peel eggs under a hard stream of cold water from the faucet.*
6. *In a bowl, combine remaining ingredients then set aside.*
7. *Chop eggs into small to medium pieces.*
8. *Add chopped eggs to the mixing bowl then stir to combine.*
9. *Adjust seasoning if desired before serving.*

SOURCE PAGE

Here are some of my favorite places to find ingredients that are not readily available at grocery stores as well as kitchen tools and supplies that help you become a better cook.

Chocosphere
P.O. Box 2237
Tualatin, OR 97062
877-992-4623

Excellent quality cocoa (Callebaut)
All Chocolates, Jimmies and sprinkles
www.chocosphere.com

Penzeys Spices
P.O. Box 924
Brookfield, WI 53045
800-741-7787

Spices, extracts, seasonings and more
www.penzeys.com

The Bakers Catalogue at King Arthur Flour
135 Route 5 South
P.O. Box 1010
Norwich, VT 05055

Silicone baking molds, pure fruit oils, citric acid, silicone spatulas, digital timers, thermometers, real truffle oil, off-set spatulas, measuring cups and spoons, knives, ice cream scoops, cheesecloth, microplane graters, cookie sheets, baking pans
www.kingarthurflour.com

Webstaurantstore.com
Professional and home kitchen items
www.webstaurantstore.com

Amazon.com
Ramekins, silicone baking molds, spatulas, pancake turners, blow torch, instant-read meat thermometer, bao buns, manual baby food grinder
www.amazon.com

Rolling Pin Kitchen Emporium
P.O. Box 21798
Long Beach, CA 90801
949-221-9399

Cheesecloth, inexpensive "harp" shaped vegetable peelers, measuring cups and spoons, knives, vast array of kitchen tools including microplane graters, blow torches, baking pans and dishes
www.rollingpin.com

Nui Enterprises
Vanilla from Tahiti
501 Chapala St. Suite A
Santa Barbara, CA 93101
805-965-5153
www.vanillafromtahiti.com

Whole Foods
550 Bowie St.
Austin, TX 78703
512-477-4455

Grains, citric acid, natural and organic products, xanthan gum, real truffle oil, miso paste
www.wholefoods.com

INDEX

FOR ALL OF MARIAN GETZ'S
COOKBOOKS AS WELL AS
COOKWARE, APPLIANCES, CUTLERY
AND KITCHEN ACCESSORIES
BY WOLFGANG PUCK

**PLEASE VISIT
HSN.COM
(KEYWORD: WOLFGANG PUCK)**